BURGERS

First published in Australia in 2010 by
New Holland Publishers (Australia) Pty Ltd
Sydney • Auckland • London • Cape Town
www.newholland.com.au

1/66 Gibbes Street Chatswood NSW 2067 Australia
218 Lake Road Northcote Auckland New Zealand
86 Edgware Road London W2 2EA United Kingdom
80 McKenzie Street Cape Town 8001 South Africa

A record of this book is available at the National Library of Australia

ISBN: 9781742570952

Publisher: Diane Jardine
Publishing manager: Lliane Clarke
Senior editor: Mary Trewby
Design: Emma Gough
Photographer: Karen Watson
Stylist: Kathy McKinnon
Production manager: Olga Dementiev
Printer: Toppan Leefung Printing Ltd (China)

NEW HOLLAND

MARIAN & PETER KISSNER

BURGERS

L 206,540/641. 66

BEEF

Beef Burger	10
Beef & Blue	12
Francois Beef	14
Spanish Beef	16
Madras Beef	17
Hawaiian Beef	18
Kangaroo—The Oz	20
Italian Beef	22
Indian Beef	24
Cajun Beef	26
Croatian Beef	27
Wagyu Beef	28
Mexican Beef	30
Moroccan Beef	32
Swedish Beef	34
Tuscan Beef	35
Portobello Beef	36
Rendang Beef	38
Yankee	40

LAMB

Lamb Burger	44
Rosemary Lamb	46
Greek Lamb	48
Cypriot Lamb	50
Cantonese Lamb	52
Balkan Lamb	54

PORK

Pork Burger	58
Chilli Pork	60
Pork with Sun-dried Tomato	62

CHICKEN

Chicken Burger	66
Caesar Chicken	68
Chilli Chicken	70
Satay Chicken	72
Turkey	74
Teriyaki Chicken	76
Portuguese Chicken	77
Moroccan Chicken	78
Thai Chicken	80
Tandoori Chicken	82
North African Chicken	84

FISH & VEGETABLES

Fish Burger	88
Prawn Burger	90
Chickpea Burger	92
Eggplant (Aubergine) Burger	94
Tofu Burger	96

CONTENTS

INTRODUCTION

In many of these burgers, the special flavours are in the patty and not simply in a sauce that goes on top. Other recipes have a basic meat patty with the toppings added to create different styles.

Most of the recipes in the following pages are based on using 500g (17oz) of the main ingredient—that is, beef, chicken, lamb, pork, fish or the featured vegetable—and make six patties for an average eater (or four for big eaters). When making cocktail-size burgers, work out how many you need at 50g (1¾oz) and multiply the quantity accordingly.

When buying the meat, fish and chicken for burgers, always get the best you can afford, but keep in mind that the leanest is not always the best—you do want some fat, for added flavour.

For a home-made look, shape the burger patties by hand.

To make a professional-looking burger, use an egg ring, available in different sizes from most supermarkets, to create a round flat patty. The formed patties can then be placed on a tray lined with baking paper and put in the freezer. When they are fully frozen, wrap them individually in freezer bags so they are ready to use whenever you feel like a burger. The frozen patty can then be cooked directly from the freezer without defrosting—in fact, cooking them straight out of the freezer on a hot barbecue or frying pan helps keep the moisture in the patty, ensuring a great-tasting, juicy burger.

Most burgers will take about three to four minutes on each side to cook. Adjust the time according to the size of the patty, but the most important things are to make sure that the plate is hot and try not to turn the patty more than once.

In the following pages, we have started each section with the basic beef, chicken, lamb, pork and vegetarian burgers, moving onto different styles, including variations on the basic, and finishing with recipes for all the sauces and condiments to go with the burgers.

With the basic burgers—or any burger for that matter—you can of course add any extra that takes your fancy: cheese, bacon, egg, beetroot, pineapple, and so on.

Rather than give you endless recipes for various seasonings, it is suggested that you use ready-made and easily obtainable seasonings.

BEEF

BEEF BURGER

THE PATTIES
55g (2oz) tomato paste
1 egg
1 tsp soy sauce
1 tsp worcestershire sauce
500g (17oz) beef mince
250g (8oz) onions, finely
  chopped
25g (¾oz) breadcrumbs
2 tsp hamburger seasoning

THE BURGERS
6 damper rolls
1 iceberg lettuce, shredded
mayonnaise (see page 124)
2 tomatoes, sliced
tomato basil relish (see page
  125)
caramelised onions (see page
  120)

Whisk together the tomato paste, egg, soy and worcestershire sauces in a bowl. Add the mince, onions, breadcrumbs and seasoning and mix until well combined. Shape the mixture into six patties, place on a hot oiled barbecue or pan and cook for 3 to 4 minutes each side.

Halve and toast the rolls, top one half with shredded lettuce, a squeeze of mayonnaise, sliced tomatoes and a beef patty. Spread over some tomato basil relish and top with caramelised onion. Finish with the other half of the roll.

BEEF & BLUE

THE PATTIES

55g (2oz) tomato paste
1 egg
1 tsp soy sauce
1 tsp worcestershire sauce
500g (17oz) beef mince
250g (8oz) onions, finely
   chopped
25g (¾oz) breadcrumbs
2 tsp hamburger seasoning
75g (2½oz) blue cheese

THE BURGERS

6 foccacio roils
1 cos lettuce
mayonnaise (see page 124)
2 tomatoes, sliced
caramelised onions (see page
   120)
1 nashi pear, thinly sliced

Whisk together the tomato paste, egg, soy and worcestershire sauces in a bowl. Add the mince, onions, breadcrumbs and seasoning and mix until well combined. Divide the mixture into 12. On a benchtop, shape each portion into a circle. Place 15g (½oz) blue cheese in the middle of each of six of the circles and then lay the remaining circles on top. Gently pinch the edges together and tamp the patties closed. Place on a hot oiled barbecue or pan and cook for 3 to 4 minutes each side.

Halve and toast the rolls. Top one half with a couple of cos leaves, a squeeze of mayonnaise, sliced tomatoes and the patty. Spread with some caramelised onion, a few slices of the pear and top with the other half roll.

FRANCOIS BEEF

The patties

55g (2oz) tomato paste
1 egg
1 tsp soy sauce
1 tsp worcestershire sauce
500g (17oz) beef mince
250g (8oz) onions, finely
   chopped
25g (¾oz) breadcrumbs
2 tsp hamburger seasoning

The burgers

6 small baguettes
1 baby cos lettuce
mayonnaise (see page 124)
2 tomatoes, sliced
caramelised onions (see page
   120)
12 slices brie cheese
2 avocados, seeded and sliced

Whisk together the tomato paste, egg, soy and worcestershire sauces in a bowl. Add the mince, onions, breadcrumbs and seasoning and mix until well combined. Divide the mixture into six, shape into a sausage shape and then flatten it to roughly the size of the baguettes. Place on a hot oiled barbecue or pan and cook for 3 to 4 minutes each side.

Halve and toast the baguettes. On one half arrange three to four baby cos leaves, a squeeze of mayonnaise, sliced tomatoes and the patty. Top with the caramelised onion, two slices of brie cheese and finish with two to three slices of avocado and the other baguette half.

SPANISH BEEF

THE PATTIES

½ red capsicum (pepper)
1 egg
55g (2oz) tomato paste
1 tsp soy sauce
1 tsp worcestershire sauce
½ tsp salt
500g (17oz) beef mince
250g (8oz) onions, finely chopped
35g (1oz) breadcrumbs
1 tsp paprika
1 tsp dried oregano

THE BURGERS

6 crusty rolls
100g (3½oz) rocket (arugula)
paprika mayonnaise (see page 124)
18 oven-roasted tomatoes (see page 121)
red onion, sliced

Quarter the capsicum, remove the membrane and seeds, dice and set aside. Whisk together the egg, tomato paste, soy and worcestershire sauces and salt in a bowl. Add the mince, onions, breadcrumbs, paprika, dried oregano and diced capsicum. Mix until well combined. Shape the mixture into six patties, place on a hot oiled barbecue or pan and cook for 3 to 4 minutes each side.

Halve and toast the rolls. Top one half with some rocket, a squeeze of paprika mayonnaise and a patty. Spread over the roasted tomatoes and slices of red onion. Finish with the other half of the roll.

MADRAS BEEF

THE PATTIES

1 egg
55g (2oz) tomato paste
100g (3½oz) madras curry
  paste
1 tsp salt
500g (17oz) beef mince
250g (8oz) onions, finely
  chopped
40g (1½oz) breadcrumbs

THE BURGERS

12 naan bread
1 cucumber, peeled and
  ribboned with the peeler
plain yoghurt
1 tomato, sliced
mango chutney (hot or mild)

Whisk together the egg, tomato paste, curry paste and salt in a bowl. Add the mince, onions and breadcrumbs and mix until well combined. Shape the mixture into six patties, place on a hot oiled barbecue or pan and cook for 3 to 4 minutes each side.

Cut the naan into 12 circles the same size as the patties and warm them. On one circle of naan arrange two or three ribbons of cucumber, a dollop of yoghurt, two slices of tomato and the patty. Top with some mango chutney and finish with another circle of naan.

HAWAIIAN BEEF

The patties

55g (2oz) tomato paste
1 egg
1 tsp soy sauce
1 tsp worcestershire sauce
500g (17oz) beef mince
250g (8oz) onions, finely
  chopped
25g (¾oz) breadcrumbs
2 tsp hamburger seasoning

The burgers

6 burger buns
½ iceberg lettuce, torn
mayonnaise (see page 124)
2 tomatoes, sliced
barbecue mayonnaise (see
  page 124)
6 slices cheddar cheese
6 slices honey ham
12 thin slices pineapple, fresh
  or canned

Whisk together the tomato paste, egg, soy and worcestershire sauces in a bowl, add the mince, onions, breadcrumbs and seasoning and mix until well combined. Shape the mixture into six patties, place on a hot oiled barbecue or pan and cook for 3 to 4 minutes each side.

Halve and toast the buns. On one half place the torn lettuce leaves, a squeeze of mayonnaise, sliced tomatoes and the beef patty. Top with the barbecue mayo, cheddar cheese, honey ham and two slices of pineapple and the other half of the bun.

KANGAROO—THE OZ

The Patties

55g (2oz) tomato paste
1 egg
½ tsp salt
500g (17oz) kangaroo mince
250g (8oz) onions, finely
   chopped
60g (2oz) sun-dried tomatoes,
   coarsely chopped
2 sprigs basil, coarsely
   chopped
30g (1oz) breadcrumbs

The Burgers

6 damper rolls
12 slices cooked beetroot (you
   can use canned)
100g (3½oz) rocket (arugula)
mayonnaise (see page 124)
2 tomatoes, sliced
caramelised onions (see page
   120)
Oz relish (see page 126)

Whisk together the tomato paste, egg and salt in a bowl. Add the mince, onions, sun-dried tomatoes, basil, breadcrumbs and mix until well combined. Shape the mixture into six patties, place on a hot oiled barbecue or pan and cook for 3 to 4 minutes each side.

Halve and toast the rolls. Arrange two slices of beetroot, some rocket, a squeeze of mayonnaise, sliced tomatoes and patty on one half. Top with caramelised onions and spread over some Oz relish and finish with the other half of the roll.

ITALIAN BEEF

THE PATTIES

55g (2oz) tomato paste
1 egg
500g (17oz) beef mince
250g (8oz) onions, finely
    chopped
2 sprigs basil, finely chopped
2 sprigs oregano, finely
    chopped
20g (½oz) breadcrumbs
30g (1oz) parmesan cheese,
    finely grated or dry

THE BURGERS

6 crusty rolls
1 baby cos lettuce
aioli (see page 118)
2 tomatoes, sliced
caramelised onions (see page
    120)
tomato sauce

Whisk together the tomato paste and egg in a bowl. Add the mince, onions, basil, oregano, breadcrumbs, parmesan and mix until well combined. Shape the mixture into six patties and place on a hot oiled barbecue or pan and cook for 3 to 4 minutes each side.

Halve and toast the rolls. Top one half with a couple of baby cos leaves, a squeeze of garlic aioli, sliced tomatoes and the beef patty. Soread some aioli, caramelised onions and tomato sauce on top and finish with the other half of the roll.

INDIAN BEEF

THE PATTIES
1 egg
1 tsp salt
50g (1¾oz) tomato paste
½ tsp cumin
½ tsp turmeric
½ tsp chilli powder
1 tsp ground cardamom
500g (17oz) beef mince
250g (8oz) onions, finely
   chopped
30g (1oz) breadcrumbs

THE BURGERS
12 naan
1 baby cos lettuce
natural yoghurt
2 tomatoes, sliced
caramelised onions (see page
   120)
dahl (see page 121)

Whisk together the egg, salt, tomato paste, cumin, turmeric, chilli powder and cardamom in a bowl. Add the mince, onions and breadcrumbs and mix until well combined. Form into six patties and cook on a hot oiled barbecue or pan.

Cut the naan into 12 circles the same size as the patties and warm them. Put a couple of cos leaves on one circle of naan, a dollop of the yoghurt, slices of tomato and the patty. Top with a spoonful of dahl and some caramelised onions and finish with another circle of naan.

CAJUN BEEF

THE PATTIES
55g (2oz) tomato paste
1 egg
1 tsp soy sauce
1 tsp worcestershire sauce
500g (17oz) beef mince
250g (8oz) onions, finely
  chopped
25g (¾oz) breadcrumbs
2 tsp hamburger seasoning
2 tsp Cajun spice

THE BURGERS
6 damper rolls
½ iceberg lettuce, shredded
mayonnaise (see page 124)
2 tomatoes, sliced
tomato basil relish (see page
  125)
caramelised onions (see page
  120)
6 slices tasty cheese

Whisk together the tomato paste, egg, soy and worcestershire sauces in a bowl. Add the mince, onions, breadcrumbs and seasoning and mix until well combined. Spread it out on a benchtop and evenly sprinkle over the Cajun spice and combine. Shape the mixture into six patties, place on a hot oiled barbecue or pan and cook for 3 to 4 minutes each side.

Halve and toast the rolls. Top one half with shredded lettuce, a squeeze of mayonnaise, sliced tomatoes and the beef patty. Spread over some tomato basil relish and top with caramelised onion, the cheese and finish with the other half of the roll.

CROATIAN BEEF

THE PATTIES

1 egg
1 clove garlic, crushed
1 tsp paprika
½ tsp cayenne pepper
1 tsp salt
250g (8oz) beef mince
125g (¾oz) pork mince
125g (¾oz) lamb mince
250g (8oz) onions, finely
  chopped
25g (¾oz) breadcrumbs

THE BURGERS

6 crusty rolls
½ iceberg lettuce
mayonnaise (see page 124)
2 tomatoes, sliced
2 red onions, sliced
hot ketchup

Whisk the egg with the garlic, paprika, cayenne pepper and salt in a bowl. Add the three minces, the onions and breadcrumbs and mix well. Shape the mixture into six patties and place on a hot oiled barbecue or pan and cook for 3 to 4 minutes each side.

Halve and toast the rolls. Top one half with lettuce leaves, a squeeze of mayonnaise, sliced tomatoes and the patty. Top with slices of red onion, a squeeze of hot ketchup and the other half of the roll.

WAGYU BEEF

The patties

1 egg
500g (17oz) wagyu beef mince
250g (8oz) onions, coarsely
  chopped
35g (1oz) breadcrumbs
4 sprigs flatleaf parsley,
  coarsely chopped
½ tsp salt

The burgers

6 crusty rolls
100g (3½oz) rocket (arugula)
mayonnaise (see page 124)
2 tomatoes, sliced
caramelised onions (see page
  120)
6 slices provolone cheese

Whisk the egg in a bowl, add all the other ingredients and mix well. Shape into six patties. Place on a hot oiled barbecue or pan and cook for 3 to 4 minutes each side.

Halve and toast the bread rolls. On one half, place some rocket, a squeeze of mayonnaise, sliced tomatoes and a wagyu patty. Top with the provolone cheese and spread over caramelised onions. Finish with the other half of the roll.

Wagyu beef is generally not available in supermarkets but can be found in specialty butchers. This recipe has fewer ingredients than regular beef burgers because the wagyu mince has so much flavour on its own.

MEXICAN BEEF

THE PATTIES
55g (2oz) tomato paste
1 egg
1 tsp soy sauce
1 tsp worcestershire sauce
500g (17oz) beef mince
250g (8oz) onions, finely
  chopped
25g (¾oz) breadcrumbs
2 tsp hamburger seasoning

THE BURGERS
6 crusty rolls
100g (3½oz) rocket (arugula)
mayonnaise (see page 124)
2 tomatoes, sliced
refried beans
guacamole (see page 121)
jalapenos

Whisk together the tomato paste, egg, soy and worcestershire sauces in a bowl. Add the mince, onions, breadcrumbs and seasoning and mix until well combined. Spread the mixture out on a benchtop and evenly sprinkle over the hamburger seasoning and combine. Shape it into six patties, place on a hot oiled barbecue or pan and cook for 3 to 4 minutes each side.

Halve and toast the rolls. Arrange rocket, a squeeze of mayonnaise, sliced tomatoes and the patty on one half. Spread over some refried bean, a spoonful of guacamole and four to six jalapeños and top with the other half of the roll.

MOROCCAN BEEF

THE PATTIES
55g (2oz) tomato paste
1 egg
1 tsp soy sauce
1 tsp worcestershire sauce
500g (17oz) beef mince
250g (8oz) onions, finely
    chopped
25g (¾oz) breadcrumbs
2 tsp hamburger seasoning
2 tsp Moroccan spice

THE BURGERS
2 long Turkish breads, cut into
    6 portions
100g (3½oz) baby spinach
mayonnaise (see page 124)
2 tomatoes, sliced
harissa (see page 122)
roasted capsicums/peppers
    (see page 126)
roasted eggplant/aubergine
    (see page 127)

Whisk together the tomato paste, egg, soy and worcestershire sauces in a bowl. Add the mince, onions, breadcrumbs and seasoning and mix until well combined. Spread the mixture out on a bench and evenly sprinkle over the Moroccan spice and combine. Shape it into six patties, place on a hot oiled barbecue or pan and cook for 3 to 4 minutes each side.

Split the bread in half and top one half with baby spinach, a squeeze of mayonnaise, sliced tomatoes and the patty. Spread over some harissa, two or three slices of roasted capsicum and three slices of roasted eggplant and finish with the other half of the bread.

SWEDISH BEEF

The patties
30cm (1¼in) slice of
   sourdough, crusts removed
150ml (5fl oz) milk
1 egg
1 tsp salt
½ tsp ground pepper
½ tsp allspice
½ tsp nutmeg, ground
500g (17oz) beef mince
250g (8oz) onions, finely
   chopped

The burgers
6 bread rolls
1 baby cos lettuce
mayonnaise
2 tomatoes, sliced
horseradish cream
caramelised onions (see page
   120)

Cut the bread into cubes and put in a bowl with the milk. Add the egg, salt, pepper, allspice, nutmeg and mash it all together with your fingers until it is almost a paste, then combine it with the mince and onions. Shape the mixture into six patties. Place on a hot oiled barbecue or pan and cook for 3 to 4 minutes each side.

Halve and toast the rolls. On one half, place a few cos leaves, a squeeze of mayonnaise, sliced tomatoes and the patty. Spread over some caramelised onions, drizzle over some horseradish cream and top with the other half of the roll.

TUSCAN BEEF

THE PATTIES
55g (2oz) tomato paste
1 egg
1 tsp soy sauce
1 tsp worcestershire sauce
500g (17oz) beef mince
250g (8oz) onions, finely
  chopped
25g (¾oz) breadcrumbs
2 tsp hamburger seasoning
1 tbsp Tuscan herbs

THE BURGERS
6 focaccia rolls
100g (3½oz) mesclun
basil mayonnaise (see page
  124)
1 cucumber, peeled and
  ribboned with the peeler
12 pieces oven-roasted tomato
  (see page 121)
6 slices provolone cheese

Whisk together the tomato paste, egg, soy and worcestershire sauces in a bowl. Add the mince, onions, breadcrumbs and seasoning and mix until well combined. Spread the mixture out on a bench and evenly sprinkle with the Tuscan herbs and combine. Shape the meat into six patties, place on a hot oiled barbecue or pan and cook for 3 to 4 minutes each side.

Halve and toast the rolls. Top one half with mesclun, a squeeze of basil mayonnaise, two or three strips of cucumber and the patty. Arrange two pieces of oven-roasted tomato and finish with a slice of provolone and the other half of the roll.

PORTOBELLO BEEF

THE PATTIES
55g (2oz) tomato paste
1 egg
1 tsp soy sauce
1 tsp worcestershire sauce
500g (17oz) beef mince
250g (8oz) onions, finely
    chopped
25g (¾oz) breadcrumbs
2 tsp hamburger seasoning

THE BURGERS
6 large field mushrooms
Tuscan seasoning
6 focaccia rolls
100g (3½oz) rocket (arugula)
6 tomatoes, sliced
avocado mayonnaise (see page
    124)
18 strips roasted capsicums/
    peppers (see page 126)

Whisk together the tomato paste, egg, soy and worcestershire sauces in a bowl. Add the mince, onions, breadcrumbs and seasoning and mix until well combined. Shape the mixture into six patties, place on a hot oiled barbecue or pan and cook for 3 to 4 minutes each side.

Remove the stems from the mushrooms and discard. Pan-fry the mushrooms with butter and a sprinkle of Tuscan seasoning for 3 to 5 minutes on each side. Set aside on paper towel.

Halve and toast the rolls. Top one half with some rocket, sliced tomatoes, the mushroom and the beef patty. Spread over some avocado mayonnaise and top with a few strips of the roasted capsicum. Finish with the other half of the roll.

RENDANG BEEF

THE PATTIES
55g (2oz) tomato paste
1 egg
1 tsp soy sauce
1 tsp worcestershire sauce
500g (17oz) beef mince
250g (8oz) onions, finely
   chopped
25g (¾oz) breadcrumbs
2 tsp hamburger seasoning
1 tsp curry powder
50g (1¾oz) shredded coconut
2 tsp brown sugar

THE BURGERS
6 bread rolls
150g (5oz) bean sprouts
mayonnaise (see page 124)
2 tomatoes, sliced
6 eggs, fried
Rendang sauce (see page 125)

Whisk together the tomato paste, egg, soy and worcestershire sauces in a bowl. Add the mince, onions, breadcrumbs and seasoning and mix until well combined. Mix together the curry powder, coconut and brown sugar in a bowl. Spread the patty mixture out on a bench and evenly sprinkle over the curry and coconut mixture and combine. Shape the meat into six patties, place on a hot oiled barbecue or pan and cook for 3 to 4 minutes each side.

Halve and toast the rolls. Top one half with bean sprouts, mayonnaise, sliced tomatoes and the patty. Top with a fried egg and pour over a little of the Rendang sauce. Finish with the other half of the roll.

YANKEE BEEF

THE PATTIES

55g (2oz) tomato paste
1 egg
1 tsp soy sauce
1 tsp worcestershire sauce
500g (17oz) beef mince
250g (8oz) onions, finely
  chopped
25g (¾oz) breadcrumbs
2 tsp hamburger seasoning

THE BURGERS

6 burger buns
½ head iceberg lettuce
mayonnaise (see page 124)
2 tomatoes, sliced
6 slices tasty cheese
12 rashers bacon, fried
American mustard
tomato sauce
12 slices dill pickle

Whisk together the tomato paste, egg, soy and worcestershire sauces in a bowl, add the mince, onions, breadcrumbs and seasoning and mix until well combined. Shape the mixture into six patties, place on a hot oiled barbecue or pan and cook for 3 to 4 minutes each side.

Halve and toast the buns. Top one half with lettuce, a squeeze of mayonnaise, sliced tomatoes and a patty. Arrange a slice of cheese and two bacon rashers on top. Top with some American mustard and tomato sauce and finish with the dill pickle and the other half of the bun.

LAMB

LAMB BURGER

1 egg
½ tsp salt
2 tbsp tomato paste
2 tbsp sun-dried tomato pesto
500g (17oz) lamb mince
250g (8oz) onions, finely
   chopped
zest of ½ lemon, finely
   chopped
4 sprigs mint, finely chopped
4 sprigs parsley, finely chopped
30g (1oz) breadcrumbs

THE BURGERS
6 focaccia rolls
1 cos lettuce
mayonnaise (see page 124)
2 tomatoes, sliced
tzatziki (see page 120)
caramelised onions (see page
   120)

Whisk the egg, salt, tomato paste and sun-dried tomato pesto in a bowl. Add the mince, onions, lemon zest, mint, parsley and breadcrumbs and mix until well combined. Shape the mixture into six patties. Place on a hot oiled barbecue or pan and cook for 3 to 4 minutes each side.

Halve and toast the rolls. Top one half with a few lettuce leaves, a squeeze of mayonnaise, sliced tomatoes and the lamb patty. Spread over some tzatziki and top with caramelised onion.

ROSEMARY LAMB

THE PATTIES

1 egg
1 tsp salt
500g (17oz) lamb mince
1 clove garlic, crushed
250g (8oz) onions, finely
  chopped
30g (1oz) breadcrumbs
3 sprigs rosemary, finely
  chopped
2 sprigs oregano, finely
  chopped

THE BURGERS

6 focaccia rolls
1 baby cos lettuce
mayonnaise (see page 124)
2 tomatoes, sliced
mint jelly (see page 123)

Whisk the egg and salt in a bowl. Add the mince, garlic, onions, breadcrumbs, rosemary and oregano and mix until well combined. Form into six patties and place on a hot oiled barbecue or pan and cook for 3 to 4 minutes on each side.

Halve and toast the rolls. On one half lay some baby cos leaves and a squeeze of mayonnaise, a couple of slices of tomato and the patty. Spread over some mint jelly and finish with the other half of the roll.

GREEK LAMB

THE PATTIES

1 egg
½ tsp salt
2 tbsp tomato paste
2 tbsp sun-dried tomato pesto
500g (17oz) lamb mince
250g (8oz) onions, finely
    chopped
zest of ½ lemon, finely
    chopped
4 sprigs mint, finely chopped
4 sprigs parsley, finely chopped
30g (1oz) breadcrumbs

THE BURGERS

6 Turkish rolls
200g (7oz) mesclun
mayonnaise (see page 124)
2 tomatoes, sliced
12 strips roasted capsicums/
    peppers (see page 126)
baba ganoush (see page 118)
12 black or green olives, pitted
    and finely sliced

Whisk the egg, salt, tomato paste and sun-dried tomato pesto in a bowl. Add the mince, onions, lemon zest, mint, parsley and breadcrumbs and mix until well combined. Shape the mixture into six patties. Place on a hot oiled barbecue or pan and cook for 3 to 4 minutes each side.

Halve and toast the rolls. Top one half with some mesclun, a squeeze of mayonnaise, sliced tomatoes and the lamb patty. Spread with some baba ganoush, a few strips of capsicum and slices of black or green olives. Finish with the other half of the bread.

CYPRIOT LAMB

THE PATTIES

1 egg
½ tsp salt
2 tbsp tomato paste
2 tbsp sun-dried tomato pesto
500g (17oz) lamb mince
250g (8oz) onions, finely
  chopped
zest of ½ lemon, finely
  chopped
4 sprigs mint, finely chopped
4 sprigs parsley, finely chopped
30g (1oz) breadcrumbs

THE BURGERS

6 Turkish rolls
100g (3½oz) baby spinach
mayonnaise
360g (12oz) fetta cheese
12 oven-roasted tomatoes (see
  page 121)
12 slices red onion

Whisk the egg, salt, tomato paste and sun-dried tomato pesto in a bowl. Add the mince, onions, lemon zest, mint, parsley and breadcrumbs and mix until well combined. Shape the mixture into six patties. Place on a hot oiled barbecue or pan and cook for 3 to 4 minutes each side.

Halve and toast the rolls. Top one half with baby spinach, a squeeze of mayonnaise and the patty. Spread over two pieces of roasted tomato, crumbled fetta cheese and a couple of slices of red onion. Finish with the other half of the bread.

CANTONESE LAMB

THE PATTIES
½ stick lemongrass
1 egg
1 tsp soy sauce
1 tsp sesame oil
1 tsp hoisin sauce
500g (17oz) lamb mince
250g (8oz) onions, finely
 chopped
30g (1oz) breadcrumbs

THE BURGERS
6 crusty rolls
100g (3½oz) rocket (arugula)
mayonnaise (see page 124)
2 tomatoes, sliced
Cantonese sauce (see page
 119)

Finely chop the soft white part of the lemongrass. Whisk the egg, soy sauce, sesame oil and hoisin sauce in a bowl. Stir in the chopped lemongrass, then add the mince, onions and breadcrumbs and mix until well combined. Form into six patties and place on a hot oiled barbecue or pan and cook for 3 to 4 minutes on each side.

Halve and toast the rolls. Top one half with some rocket, a squeeze of mayonnaise, sliced tomatoes and the patty. Spread over some Cantonese sauce and finish with the other half of the roll.

BALKAN LAMB

The Patties

1 egg
2 cloves garlic, crushed
1 tsp cumin
1 tsp salt
500g (17oz) lamb mince
250g (8oz) onions, finely
   chopped
6 sprigs parsley, chopped
3 stems coriander/cilantro
   (roots and leaves), chopped
30g (1oz) breadcrumbs

The Burgers

6 Turkish rolls
100g (3½oz) mesclun
mayonnaise (see page 124)
2 tomatoes, sliced
roasted capsicums/peppers
   (see page 126)
red onions, sliced, to taste

Whisk the egg, crushed garlic, cumin and salt in a bowl. Add the lamb mince, onions, parsley, coriander and breadcrumbs and mix until well combined. Form into six patties. Place on a hot oiled barbecue or pan and cook for 3 to 4 minutes on each side.

Halve and toast the rolls. Top one half with mesclun, a squeeze of mayonnaise, sliced tomatoes, the patty and a few slices of roasted capsicum. Finish with sliced red onion.

PORK

PORK BURGER

THE PATTIES

1 egg

2 tsp teriyaki sauce

1 tsp salt

500g (17oz) pork mince

250g (8oz) onions, finely
chopped

1 medium green apple,
coarsely grated

4cm (1½in) knob ginger, finely
grated

30g (1oz) breadcrumbs

THE BURGERS

6 crusty rolls

12 slices cooked beetroot (you
could use canned)

100g (3½oz) baby spinach
leaves

1 cucumber, peeled and cut
into ribbons

apple sauce (see page 118)

caramelised onions (see page
120)

Whisk the egg, teriyaki sauce and salt in a bowl.
Add the mince, onions, grated apple, ginger
and breadcrumbs and mix until well combined.
Shape the mixture into six patties and place on
a hot oiled barbecue or pan and cook for 3 to 4
minutes each side.

Halve and toast the rolls. On one half place a
couple of slices of beetroot, some baby spinach
and cucumber ribbons and the patty. Spread
over some caramelised onions and top with
apple sauce and the other half of the roll.

CHILLI PORK

The patties

1 egg
50ml (1¾fl oz) sweet chilli
   sauce
1 tsp salt
500g (17oz) pork mince
250g (8oz) onion, finely
   chopped
1 long red chilli, finely chopped
3 stems coriander/cilantro
   (roots and leaves), finely
   chopped
30g (1oz) breadcrumbs

The burgers

6 damper rolls
100g (3½oz) baby spinach
100g (3½oz) bean sprouts
mayonnaise (see page 124)
12 strips roasted capsicums/
   peppers (see page 126)
3 long red chillies, seeded and
   cut into strips
tamarind sauce (see page 126)

Whisk together the egg, sweet chilli sauce and salt in a bowl. Add the mince, onions, chilli, coriander and breadcrumbs and mix until well combined. Shape the mixture into six patties and place on a hot oiled barbecue or pan and cook for 3 to 4 minutes each side.

Halve and toast the rolls. On one half spread some baby spinach and bean sprouts, a squeeze of mayonnaise, then top with the patty. Drizzle on some tamarind sauce, add a couple of strips of roasted capsicum and a few strips of the red chilli. Finish with the other half of the roll.

PORK WITH SUN-DRIED TOMATO

THE PATTIES

1 egg
1 tsp salt
500g (17oz) pork mince
250g (8oz) onions, finely
  chopped
150g (5oz) sun-dried tomatoes,
  finely chopped
30g (1oz) breadcrumbs
4 sprigs basil, coarsely
  chopped

THE BURGERS

6 focaccia rolls
100g (3½oz) mesclun
mayonnaise (see page 124)
2 tomatoes, sliced
capsicum (pepper) chutney
  (see page 119)
caramelised onions (see page
  120)

Whisk together the egg and salt in a bowl. Add the mince, onions, sun-dried tomatoes, breadcrumbs and basil. Mix until well combined. Shape the mixture into six patties and place on a hot oiled barbecue or pan and cook for 3 to 4 minutes each side.

Halve and toast the rolls. On one half arrange some mesclun and a squeeze of mayonnaise, a couple of slices of tomato and the patty. Spread over some capsicum chutney and top with caramelised onions and the other half of the roll.

For all the chicken burgers, thigh mince is used. Because the final mixture is fairly wet and difficult to form into patties, it is a good idea to form them on a sheet of greaseproof or baking paper using egg rings, as described in the Introduction. Place the patties in the freezer for about 1 hour, until firm to the touch, before cooking. If you don't have time to do this, you can spoon the mixture directly onto the hotplate and cook them for 2 to 3 minutes on each side, depending on the thickness of the patties. If you are using frozen patties, cook for another minute on each side.

CHICKEN

CHICKEN BURGER

THE PATTIES

100g (3½oz) rice
150g (5oz) zucchini (courgettes)
1 egg, whisked
2 tbsp tomato paste
1 tsp soy sauce
1 tsp worcestershire sauce
1 tsp kecap manis
½ tsp salt
500g (17oz) chicken thigh
    mince

THE BURGERS

6 damper rolls
½ iceberg lettuce, shredded
mayonnaise (see page 124)
2 tomatoes, sliced
salsa verde (see page 125)
caramelised onions (see page
    120)

Cook the rice until tender, about 10 to 12 minutes, drain and allow to cool. Shred the zucchini in a food processor or with a coarse grater and, using a cloth or tea towel, squeeze out as much liquid as possible; set aside.

Whisk together the egg, tomato paste, soy and worcestershire sauces, kecap manis and salt in a bowl. Add the chicken mince, rice, zucchini and mix until well combined. Form the mixture into six patties and cook on a hot oiled barbecue or pan.

Halve and toast the rolls. Top one half with lettuce, a squeeze of mayonnaise, sliced tomatoes and the chicken patty. Spread over some caramelised onions and salsa verde and finish with the other half of the roll.

CHICKEN CAESAR

THE PATTIES
100g (3½oz) rice
150g (5oz) zucchini (courgettes)
1 egg, whisked
2 tbsp tomato paste
1 tsp soy sauce
1 tsp worcestershire sauce
1 tsp kecap manis
½ tsp salt
500g (17oz) chicken thigh
  mince

THE BURGERS
4–5 hard-boiled eggs, cooled
  and shelled
6 rashers bacon
2 long Turkish breads, cut into
  6 portions
1 baby cos lettuce
caesar sauce (see page 119)
2 tomatoes, sliced
fresh shaved parmesan cheese

Cook the rice until tender, about 10 to 12 minutes, drain and allow to cool. Shred the zucchini in a food processor or with a coarse grater and, using a cloth or tea towel, squeeze out as much liquid as possible; set aside.

Whisk together the egg, tomato paste, soy and worcestershire sauces, kecap manis and salt in a bowl. Add the chicken mince, rice, zucchini and mix until well combined. Form the mixture into six patties and cook on a hot oiled barbecue or pan.

Cut the eggs into about 18–20 slices. Cut the bacon rashers in half and fry them to taste and place on kitchen towel to drain excess fat.

Split the bread in half and toast. On one half, arrange two to three baby cos leaves, squeeze on some caesar sauce and top with sliced tomatoes and the chicken patty. Top with two slices of bacon, three or four slices of egg, more caesar sauce and some parmesan cheese. Finish with the other half of the bread.

CHILLI CHICKEN

THE PATTIES
100g (3½oz) rice
1 egg
50g (1¾oz) sweet chilli sauce
½ tsp soy sauce
½ tsp salt
500g (17oz) chicken thigh
   mince
25g (¾oz) breadcrumbs
3 stems coriander/cilantro
   (roots and leaves), finely
   chopped

THE BURGERS
6 bread rolls
100g (3½oz) baby spinach
 mayonnaise (see page 124)
100g (3½oz) bean sprouts
1 cucumber, peeled and cut
   into ribbons
2 long red chillies, cut into
   strips
fresh lime juice

Cook the rice until tender, about 10 to 12 minutes, drain and allow to cool.

Whisk together the egg, sweet chilli and soy sauces and salt in a bowl. Add the chicken mince, rice, breadcrumbs and coriander. Mix until well combined. Form into six patties and cook on a hot oiled barbecue or pan.

Halve and toast the rolls. Top one half with baby spinach, a squeeze of mayonnaise, a few bean sprouts, two or three ribbons of cucumber and the chilli patty. Garnish with a few strips of chilli and a squeeze of lime juice and top with the other half of the roll.

SATAY CHICKEN

THE PATTIES

100g (3½oz) rice
150g (5oz) zucchini (courgettes)
1 egg, whisked
2 tbsp tomato paste
1 tsp soy sauce
1 tsp worcestershire sauce
1 tsp kecap manis
½ tsp salt
500g (17oz) chicken thigh
    mince
150g (5oz) satay paste

THE BURGERS

6 bread rolls
100g (3½oz) bean sprouts
mayonnaise (see page 124)
2 tomatoes, sliced
1 cucumber, peeled and cut
    into ribbons
caramelised onions

Cook the rice until tender, about 10 to 12 minutes, drain and allow to cool. Shred the zucchini in a food processor or with a coarse grater and, using a cloth or tea towel, squeeze out as much liquid as possible; set aside.

Whisk together the egg, tomato paste, soy and worcestershire sauces, kecap manis and salt in a bowl. Add the chicken mince, rice, zucchini, and satay paste and mix until well combined. Form the mixture into six patties and cook on a hot oiled barbecue or pan.

Halve and toast the rolls. Top one half with bean sprouts, some mayonnaise, sliced tomatoes, two or three ribbons of cucumber and the satay patty. Top with some caramelised onions and finish with the other half of the roll.

TURKEY

The patties
1 egg
½ tsp salt
500g (17oz) turkey mince
250g (8oz) onions, finely
  chopped
20g (1½oz) dried cranberries,
  finely chopped
30g (1oz) breadcrumbs
25g (¾oz) walnuts, coarsely
  chopped
3 sprigs parsley, finely chopped
3 sprigs sage, finely chopped

The burgers
6 herbed focaccia rolls
100g (3½oz) mesclun
mayonnaise (see page 124)
1 tomato, sliced
cranberry sauce
1 avocado, sliced

Whisk together the egg and salt in a bowl.
Add the turkey mince, onions, cranberries,
breadcrumbs, walnuts, parsley and sage.
Combine well. Form into six patties and cook on
a hot oiled barbecue or pan.

Halve and toast the rolls. Top one half with
mesclun, some mayonnaise, sliced tomatoes and
the patty. Spread over some cranberry sauce and
top with two or three slices of avocado and the
other half of the roll.

TERIYAKI CHICKEN

THE PATTIES

100g (3½oz) rice
150g (5oz) zucchini (courgettes)
½ bunch shallots
1 egg, whisked
2 tsp teriyaki sauce
½ tsp salt
¼ tsp freshly ground black
*   pepper*
500g (17oz) chicken thigh
*   mince*

THE BURGERS

½ bunch shallots
6 crusty rolls
100g (3½oz) rocket (arugula)
mayonnaise (see page 124)
2 tomatoes, sliced
1 cucumber, peeled and cut
*   into ribbons*
natural yoghurt
lime juice

Cook the rice until soft, about 10 to 12 minutes, drain and allow to cool. Shred the zucchini in a food processor or with a coarse grater and, using a cloth or tea towel, squeeze out as much liquid as possible. Cut the roots and the soft green ends off the shallots and then finely chop the white parts.

Whisk together the egg, teriyaki sauce, salt and ground black pepper in a bowl. Add the chicken mince, rice, zucchini and shallots and combine well. Form the mixture into six patties and cook on a hot oiled barbecue or pan.

Prepare the shallots as for the patties. Halve and toast the rolls. Top one half with rocket, some mayonnaise, sliced tomatoes, two or three ribbons of cucumber and the teriyaki patty. Spread over some yoghurt and shallots. Finish with a squeeze of lime juice and the other half of the roll.

PORTUGUESE CHICKEN

The patties
100g (3½oz) rice
150g (5oz) zucchini (courgettes)
1 egg, whisked
2 tbsp tomato paste
1 tsp soy sauce
1 tsp piri piri
½ tsp salt
500g (17oz) chicken thigh
   mince
3 sprigs oregano, finely
   chopped

The burgers
6 crusty rolls
1 baby cos lettuce
mayonnaise (see page 124)
2 tomatoes, sliced
chilli jam (see page 120)
caramelised onions (see page
   120)
6 slices provolone cheese

Cook the rice until soft, about 10 to 12 minutes, drain and allow to cool. Shred the zucchini in a food processor or with a coarse grater and, using a cloth or tea towel, squeeze out as much liquid as possible.

Whisk together the egg, tomato paste, soy, piri piri and salt in a bowl. Add the chicken mince, rice, zucchini and oregano and combine well. Form the mixture into six patties and cook on a hot oiled barbecue or pan.

Halve and toast the rolls. Top one half with some baby cos leaves, a little mayonnaise, a couple of slices of tomato and the patty. Spread with some chilli jam and caramelised onions and top with cheese and the other half of the roll.

MOROCCAN CHICKEN

THE PATTIES

100g (3½oz) rice
150g (5oz) zucchini (courgettes)
1 egg, whisked
2 tbsp tomato paste
1 tsp soy sauce
1 tsp worcestershire sauce
1 tsp kecap manis
½ tsp salt
500g (17oz) chicken thigh
   mince
2 tsp Moroccan seasoning

THE BURGERS

6 Turkish rolls
1 baby cos
1 red onion, sliced
2 tomatoes, sliced
smoky eggplant (aubergine)
   sauce (see page 127)

Cook the rice until tender, 10 to 12 minutes, drain and allow to cool. Shred the zucchini in a food processor or with a coarse grater and, using a cloth or tea towel, squeeze out as much liquid as possible; set aside.

Whisk together the egg, tomato paste, soy and worcestershire sauces, kecap manis and salt in a bowl. Add the chicken mince, rice, zucchini and mix until well combined. Sprinkle over the Moroccan seasoning and combine well. Form the mixture into six patties and cook on a hot oiled barbecue or pan.

Halve and toast the rolls. Lay a few baby cos leaves on one side, some slices of red onion, some sliced tomatoes, the patty and a big dollop of the smoky eggplant sauce. Finish with the other half of the roll.

THAI CHICKEN

THE PATTIES

120g (4oz) rice
150g (5oz) zucchini (courgettes)
1 egg, whisked
2 tbsp tomato paste
1 tsp soy sauce
1 tsp worcestershire sauce
1 tsp kecap manis
½ tsp salt
500g (17oz) chicken thigh
    mince
⅓ stalk lemongrass
2–3 kaffir lime leaves

THE BURGERS

6 crusty rolls
100g (3½oz) mesclun
1 medium carrot, peeled and
    cut into ribbons
Thai mayonnaise (see page
    124)
2 tomatoes, sliced
1 red onion, sliced
lime juice

Cook 100g (3½oz) of rice until tender, about 10 to 12 minutes, drain and allow to cool. Shred the zucchini in a food processor or with a coarse grater and, using a cloth or tea towel, squeeze out as much liquid as possible; set aside.

Whisk together the egg, tomato paste, soy and worcestershire sauces, kecap manis and salt in a bowl. Add the chicken mince, rice, zucchini and mix until well combined.

Toast the remaining rice in a heavy-based frying pan until golden brown, cool and then grind in a mortar and pestle or a small food processor. Chop the lemongrass very finely. Remove the spines from the kaffir lime leaves, roll up together and chop very finely. Combine the ground rice, kaffir lime leaves and lemongrass with the chicken burger mixture. Form the mixture into six patties and cook on a hot oiled barbecue or pan.

Halve and toast the roll. Top one half with mesclun, some Thai mayonnaise, a few ribbons of carrot, tomato slices and the patty. Finish with red onion, more mayonnaise, a squeeze of fresh lime juice and the other half of the roll.

TANDOORI CHICKEN

THE PATTIES
100g (3½oz) rice
150g (5oz) zucchini (courgettes)
1 egg, whisked
2 tbsp tomato paste
1 tsp soy sauce
1 tsp worcestershire sauce
1 tsp kecap manis
½ tsp salt
500g (17oz) chicken thigh
  mince
150g (5oz) tandoori paste

THE BURGERS
12 slices naan
1 baby cos lettuce
raita (see page 126)
lime pickle yoghurt (see page
  122)

Cook the rice until tender, 10 to 12 minutes, drain and allow to cool. Shred the zucchini in a food processor or with a coarse grater and, using a cloth or tea towel, squeeze out as much liquid as possible; set aside.

Whisk together the egg, tomato paste, soy and worcestershire sauces, kecap manis and salt in a bowl. Add the chicken mince, rice, zucchini and tandoori paste and mix until well combined. Form the mixture into six patties and cook on a hot oiled barbecue or pan.

Cut the naan into 12 circles the same size as the patties. Warm the naan and top one circle with some baby cos leaves, spoon on some raita, add the patty and spread over the lime pickle yoghurt. Top with another circle of naan.

NORTH AFRICAN CHICKEN

THE PATTIES

100g (3½oz) rice
150g (5oz) zucchini (courgettes)
1 egg, whisked
2 tbsp tomato paste
1 tsp soy sauce
1 tsp worcestershire sauce
1 tsp kecap manis
½ tsp salt
500g (17oz) chicken thigh
  mince
2 tsp ras el hanout (see page
  123)

THE BURGERS

6 Turkish rolls
100g (3½oz) rocket (arugula)
mayonnaise (see page 124)
2 tomatoes, sliced
hummus (see page 122)
caramelised onions (see page
  120)
lime juice

Cook the rice until tender, 10 to 12 minutes, drain and allow to cool. Shred the zucchini in a food processor or with a coarse grater and, using a cloth or tea towel, squeeze out as much liquid as possible; set aside.

Whisk together the egg, tomato paste, soy and worcestershire sauces, kecap manis and salt in a bowl. Add the chicken mince, rice, zucchini and mix until well combined. Sprinkle over the ras el hanout and combine well. Form the mixture into six patties and cook on a hot oiled barbecue or pan.

Halve and toast the rolls. On one half put some rocket, a squeeze of mayonnaise, sliced tomatoes and the patty. Spread over some caramelised onions, hummus and a squeeze of lime juice. Finish with the other half of the roll.

VEG

FISH &
ETABLES

FISH BURGER

THE PATTIES

500g (17oz) potatoes
2 tsp butter
salt and freshly ground black
  pepper
1 x 200g (7oz) can tuna in brine
1 x 200g (7oz) can pink salmon
  in brine
1 egg
2 tbsp fish sauce
½ tsp piri piri
1 clove garlic, crushed
zest of 1 lemon
30g (1oz) breadcrumbs
juice of 1 lime

THE BURGERS

6 crusty rolls
½ iceberg lettuce, shredded
mayonnaise (see page 124)
2 tomatoes, sliced
1 lime
tartare sauce (see page 127)

Boil the potatoes in salted water, drain and mash well with the butter, season with salt and pepper and set aside. Drain the tuna and salmon, remove the bones from the salmon and crumble both fish into a bowl.

Whisk together the egg, fish sauce, piri piri and crushed garlic in a bowl. Add the tuna and salmon, the mashed potatoes, lemon zest and breadcrumbs. Mix until well combined. Shape into six patties, preferably with some rings. Compress well and freeze for a better result (if you don't freeze them they will tend to fall apart). Cook the patties on a hot oiled plate for about 5 minutes on each side, squeezing on some lime juice while they are cooking.

Halve and toast the rolls. Top one half with shredded lettuce, some mayonnaise, sliced tomatoes and the fish patty. Squeeze more lime juice on the patty, spread over some tartare sauce and finish with the other half of the roll.

PRAWN

THE PATTIES

500g (17oz) green prawns,
  shelled and deveined
125g (4oz) cooked rice
½ tsp salt
juice of 1 lime
100g (3½oz) shredded coconut

THE BURGERS

6 crusty rolls
½ head iceberg lettuce,
  shredded
2 tomatoes, sliced
aioli (see page 118)

Put the prawns, cooked rice, salt and lime juice in a food processor and, using the pulse, blend just enough until everything is mashed—don't overdo it. Scrape the mixture out into a bowl and mix in the shredded coconut. Shape into six patties. Cook on a hot oiled plate for 1 to 2 minutes on each side. The prawn mixture will cook very quickly—watch them carefully so they don't dry out.

Halve and toast the rolls. On one half, arrange some shredded lettuce, mayonnaise, sliced tomatoes and the patty. Top with some aioli and the other half of the roll.

CHICKPEA

THE PATTIES

1 x 400g (14oz) can of
  chickpeas, drained
1 egg
100g (3½oz) onions, finely
  chopped
4 sprigs mint, coarsely
  chopped
4 sprigs flatleaf parsley,
  coarsely chopped
15g (½oz) flour
2 tsp ground cumin
1 tsp Moroccan seasoning
½ tsp salt

THE BURGERS

6 Turkish rolls
100g (3½oz) mesclun
mayonnaise (see page 124)
2 tomatoes, sliced
1 red onion, sliced
tahini yoghurt sauce (see page
  122)

Put all the ingredients into a blender and pulse until well combined but not smooth—leave a bit of texture in the mixture. Shape into six patties and cook on a hot oiled barbecue or pan for 2 minutes each side.

Halve and toast the rolls. Top one half with mesclun, some mayonnaise, slices of tomato and the chickpea patty. Top with a few slices of red onion, some tahini yoghurt sauce and the other half of the roll.

EGGPLANT (AUBERGINE)

THE PATTIES

1 large eggplant (aubergine)
salt
25g (¾oz) breadcrumbs
1 tbsp Moroccan seasoning
35g (1¼oz) parmesan, grated
1 tsp piri piri
50g (1¾oz) flour
3 eggs
50g (1¾oz) butter
1 tbsp olive oil

THE BURGERS

6 damper rolls
½ iceberg lettuce, shredded
mayonnaise (see page 124)
2 tomatoes, sliced
capsicum (pepper) chutney
   (see page 119)
caramelised onions (see page
   120)

Preheat the oven to 180°C (350°F). Cut the eggplant into six slices crossways, salt both sides and drain in a colander for about 20 minutes, until the eggplant sweats; wash under cold water and pat dry.

Mix together the breadcrumbs, Moroccan seasoning, parmesan and piri piri in a bowl large enough to fit each eggplant slice. Whisk the eggs in a similar size bowl and sieve the flour into another. Using a fork or skewer, first coat each eggplant slice with flour, then dip into the eggs and finally the breadcrumb mix, making sure it is well coated. Repeat with all the slices.

Put the butter and olive oil in a baking tray large enough to fit the eggplant slices in a single layer and put in the oven for long enough to melt the butter. Place the eggplant on the tray and bake for 8 to 10 minutes on each side. Remove from the oven and allow the patties to cool. They can be kept covered in the fridge for about five days.

When ready to use, place the patties on a hotplate with some oil and cook both sides until sizzling, about 2 minutes each side.

Halve and toast the rolls. Top one half with lettuce, mayonnaise, slices of tomato and the eggplant. Spread over some capsicum chutney and top with caramelised onions and the other half of the roll.

TOFU

THE PATTIES

3 blocks of firm tofu, about
   700g (24oz)
juice of ½ lime
1 tbsp sweet chilli sauce
25ml (¾fl oz) soy sauce
25ml (¾fl oz) sweet plum sauce

THE BURGERS

6 Turkish rolls
100g (3½oz) mesclun
Thai mayonnaise (see page
   124)
2 tomatoes, sliced
1 medium carrot, peeled and
   cut into ribbons
1 red onion, sliced
lime juice

Cut each block of tofu into three slices and place on a paper towel; place another paper towel on top and pat dry. Repeat this a couple of times, until the tofu slices are fairly dry, and then sit them on another piece of folded paper towel for about 15 minutes. Use a fork or skewer to perforate the tofu slices without breaking them up and place them in a shallow dish.

Whisk together the lime juice, sweet chilli, soy and sweet plum sauces in a bowl and pour over the perforated tofu slices, cover and allow them to marinate for at least 1 hour in the fridge.

Cook the tofu slices on an oiled hotplate for 2 minutes each side.

Halve and toast the rolls. On one half place mesclun, Thai mayonnaise, slices of tomato, a few ribbons of carrot and the patty. Top with a red onion, more mayonnaise, a squeeze of lime juice and the other half of the roll.

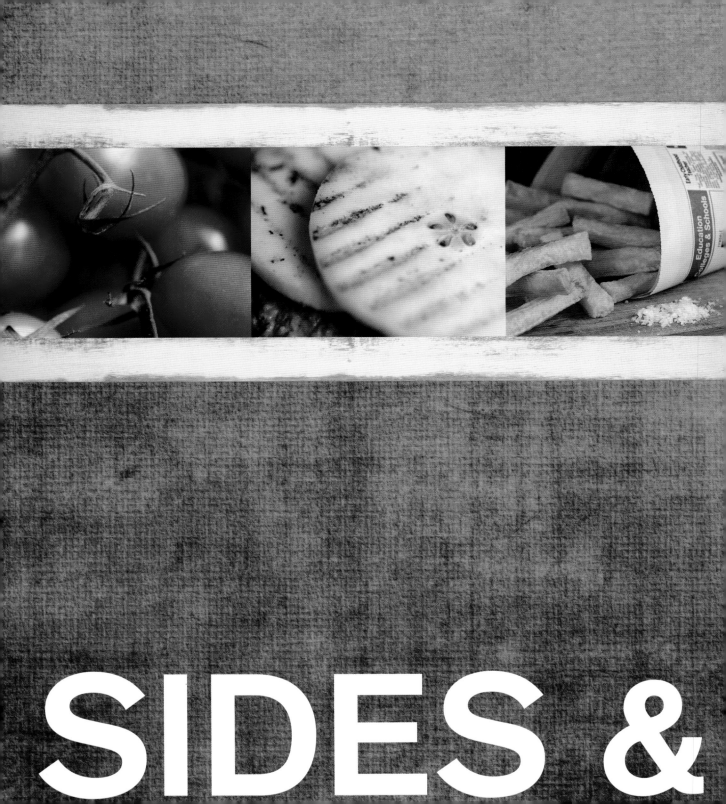

SIDES &

SALADS

BREAKFAST PIZZA FOR ONE

1 egg
4 bacon rashers
1 tortilla wrap
1 tbsp tomato basil relish (see
   page 125)
4 tomato slices
4 slices of provolone
basil leaves to garnish

Fry the egg until it has just set, making sure you don't overcook it. Set it aside and fry the bacon rashers; again don't overcook, and set them aside. Brown the tortilla on one side on a hotplate or frying pan, then turn it over. While the second side is browning, spread the toasted side with tomato basil relish.

Place the tortilla on a baking tray. Spread over tomato slices and put the fried egg in the middle. Around the egg, place the bacon and then the provolone. Put the baking tray under a hot grill and grill until the cheese has melted. Serve garnished with basil.

Serves 1

STEAK SANDWICH

6 x 150g (5oz) scotch fillet
 steaks
6 Turkish rolls
1 baby cos lettuce
2 tomatoes, sliced
mayonnaise (see page 124)
Dijon mustard
caramelised onions (see page
 120)

Have your butcher cut the steaks into 150g (5oz) (1¾oz) slices. Alternatively, buy a whole scotch fillet, wrap tightly with clingfilm and put in the freezer for an hour—this will chill the meat enough to be able to easily slice the fillet.

Cook the steak on a hot grill to your liking. Halve and toast the rolls, put some cos lettuce leaves on one half, with mayonnaise, slices of tomato and the steak. Spread over some mustard and finish with some caramelised onions and the other half of the roll.

Serves 6

THE BEST CHIPS

2 large brushed Sebago or
   other waxy potatoes, peeled
oil
sea salt and freshly ground
   black pepper
aioli (see page 118)

Cut the potatoes into 10–15mm (½in) thick strips, rinse under cold water to clean and remove the waxy feel. Pat them dry.

Heat the oil to 140°C (275°F) in a deep-fryer and cook the chips for 8 minutes. Remove, drain and place on paper towels to cool down.

Reheat the oil to 180°C (350°F) and put the chips back in the fryer for about 6 minutes, until they are golden. Remove, drain on paper towels. Sprinkle with sea salt and freshly ground pepper and serve with aioli.

COS, PARMESAN, OLIVE OIL & CARAMELISED BALSAMIC SALAD

2 baby cos lettuce
olive oil
50g (1¾oz) shaved parmesan
caramelised balsamic (see
    page 120)

Trim the outside leaves off the lettuce. Cut the lettuces through the centre and lay on a platter, cut side up, then drizzle the olive oil over the cut leaves. Lay the shaved parmesan over and drizzle the caramelised balsamic over the whole plate.

Serves 4

ZUCCHINI (COURGETTE) & WALNUT SALAD

50g (1¾oz) walnuts
1 iceberg lettuce
1 zucchini (courgettes)
50g (1¾oz) shaved parmesan
olive oil
caramelised balsamic (see
    page 120)

Dry-roast the walnuts in a frying pan until they start to colour, then set them aside to cool.

Tear the lettuce apart and toss loosely in a large salad bowl. Slice the zucchini as thin as possible and arrange over the lettuce, scatter over the toasted walnuts and top with the shaved parmesan. Sprinkle some olive oil over the salad and finish with a zigzag of caramelised balsamic.

Serves 4

NIÇOISE SALAD

100g (3½oz) green beans
1 large potato
2 eggs, soft to hard boiled
1 x 200g (7oz) can tuna
1 large vine-ripened tomato
12–20 pitted black olives
olive oil
caramelised balsamic (see
  page 120)
salt and freshly ground black
  pepper

Cut the tips off the end of the beans, cut in half and blanch in boiling water for 3 minutes, then immediately cool under cold running water.

Peel the potato and cut into 5mm (¼in) slices. Cook in boiling water until just tender, making sure you don't overcook; allow to cool.

Boil the eggs until almost hard—a slightly soft centre is ideal. Shell them when cool enough to handle and cut into quarters.

Slice the tomato into six wedges.

On an oval plate, arrange the tuna at one end, the the potatoes beside it, then the beans, the egg, the tomatoes and and finish with the olives.

Drizzle some olive oil over all the ingredients and then zigzag the caramelised balsamic over the plate. Check the seasoning and serve with thick slices of sourdough.

Serves 1

ROASTED BEETROOT & ROSEMARY SALAD

100g (3½oz) ricotta cheese
1 large raw beetroot
2 cloves garlic
2 small red onions, cut into
   wedges
olive oil
3 sprigs rosemary
200g (7oz) cherry tomatoes
   (truss tomatoes are best)
100g (3½oz) baby spinach
balsamic vinegar

Preheat the oven to 180°C (350°F) and line a baking tray with foil. Put the ricotta on a paper towel to dry a little.

Using kitchen gloves, peel and cut the beetroot into 15mm cubes. Roughly chop the garlic and put it in a bowl with the beetroot and red onions. Pour over a little olive oil and toss until the beetroot and garlic are well coated. Place on the prepared baking tray and top with the rosemary. Cover with foil and bake for about 30 minutes, until the beetroot is cooked with just a little crunch in the middle. Remove and allow to cool down.

Cut the cherry tomatoes into halves or quarters depending on size. Toss the spinach with some olive oil and balsamic vinegar in a bowl. Top with the beetroot and red onion, crumble over the ricotta, then add the tomatoes. Serve with your favourite burger.

Serves 4

SPINACH, BACON, FETTA SALAD WITH HONEY & OLIVE OIL

150g (5oz) bacon, cut into 2cm
   (¾in) dice
200g (7oz) baby spinach
200g (7oz) fetta cheese
a drizzle of honey
a drizzle of olive oil

Fry the bacon until just cooked and drain on a paper towel, taking care not to overcook it. Allow the bacon to cool down.

Toss the baby spinach in a bowl with the bacon, crumble over the fetta and toss a little more, then lightly drizzle over the honey and then the olive oil. Give it another gentle toss and serve.

Serves 4

POTATO & SWEET POTATO SALAD WITH GARLIC

THE SALAD
500g (17oz) new potatoes
300g (10oz) sweet potato
olive oil for coating
olive oil spray
4 cloves garlic, roughly
    chopped
sea salt and freshly ground
    black pepper
dressing, see below
1 bunch spring onions
    (scallions)

THE DRESSING
2 tbsp sour cream
2 tbsp mayonnaise (use a
    whole-egg mayonnaise)
2 tbsp sesame oil
½ tbsp wholegrain mustard
1 tbsp honey
½ tbsp barbecue sauce

Preheat the oven to 220°C (450°F). Cut the new potatoes in half, or quarters if they are large, then cut the sweet potato the same size. Keep the two potatoes separate.

Coat the two potatoes with some olive oil in separate bowls and spray a shallow baking tray with oil. Spread the new potatoes over the tray and bake for 15 minutes. Take the tray out of the oven and scatter over all the chopped garlic. Using a spatula, scrape and toss them around. Add the sweet pototes, sprinkle with the sea salt and freshly ground pepper and put back in the oven for another 15 minutes, until golden. Remove and allow them to cool.

Finely chop the spring onion, keeping the white and green parts separate.

For the dressing, combine all the ingredients. Mix together the two potatoes in a serving bowl, add the dressing and the white part of the spring onions. Toss and serve with the green part of the spring onions as garnish.

Serves 4

BASICS

AIOLI

200g (7oz) mayonnaise (see page 124)
2–3 heads garlic, unpeeled

Preheat the oven to 150°C (300°F). Roast the unpeeled garlic in the heated oven for 1 hour. When done, allow to cool, then squeeze the soft centre into the mayonnaise and blend together.

- -

APPLE SAUCE

2 large granny smith apples, peeled, cored and diced
125g (4oz) brown sugar
½ stick cinnamon
1 star anise
2 sprigs mint, leaves only
1 long red chilli, seeded and halved
250ml (9fl oz) water

Put all the ingredients in a saucepan. Bring to the boil, uncovered, then lower to a simmer for about 20 minutes, until the apples are soft and most of the water has evaporated. Drain and remove the star anise and cinnamon. Either puree or mash the apples, depending on whether you like a smooth or chunky sauce. The drained liquid is also nice on ice cream.

- -

BABA GANOUSH

1 large eggplant (aubergine)
1 clove garlic, thinly sliced
1 tbsp yoghurt
2 tbsp tahini
50ml (1¾fl oz) olive oil
juice of 1 lemon
sea salt and freshly ground black pepper

Preheat the oven to 180°C (350°F). Char the unpeeled eggplant over an open flame (a gas burner on your stove works well) and cut in half lengthways. Crisscross with slits, insert the sliced garlic into the slits and bake for 20 minutes at 180°C (350°F) and then lower the oven to 150°C (300°F) and bake for another 10 minutes, or a little more if the eggplant is not completely soft.

Allow to cool, scoop the flesh out of the skin and put into a food processor. Blend until smooth, then slowly add the yoghurt, tahini, olive oil and lemon juice. Season with salt and pepper to taste.

CAESAR SAUCE

1 egg
50ml (1¾fl oz) white wine vinegar
150ml (5fl oz) vegetable oil
1½ tbsp mayonnaise (see page 124)
1 tbsp worcestershire sauce
2 tbsp parmesan cheese, grated
½ tsp caster sugar
¼ tsp white pepper
1 tsp Dijon mustard
1 anchovy fillet (optional)

Whisk all the ingredients together in a blender.

CANTONESE SAUCE

200ml (7fl oz) sweet chilli sauce
½ bunch coriander (cilantro), coarsely
  chopped
juice of ½ lime
2cm (¾in) knob ginger, finely grated

Combine all the ingredients in a bowl with a spoon.

CAPSICUM (PEPPER) CHUTNEY

2 large red capsicums (peppers), roasted
  (see page 126)
2 cloves garlic, crushed
1 onion, finely chopped
1 tsp grated fresh ginger
1 tsp salt
250g (8oz) brown sugar
250ml (8fl oz) balsamic vinegar

Dice the flesh of the roasted capsicums and add to a saucepan with the remaining ingredients. Bring to the boil, uncovered, and then simmer for about 30 minutes, until a chutney-like consistency is reached.

Pour into sterilised bottles and seal.

CARAMELISED BALSAMIC

1ltr (34fl oz) balsamic vinegar
100g (3½oz) dark brown sugar

Put the balsamic and the sugar in a heavy-based saucepan and bring to the boil. Lower the heat to a slow simmer and reduce by two-thirds—this should take about 60–90 minutes. You should have about 350ml of thick caramelised balsamic glaze.

CARAMELISED ONIONS

2 large onions
1 tbsp olive oil
salt

Heat the olive oil in a heavy-based frying pan. Add the onions and get them sizzling, then turn the heat to low, stirring the onions. Sprinkle with salt and keep stirring until the onions begin to change colour and caramelise.

CHILLI JAM

2 red capsicums (peppers), seeded and
    chopped
2 long red chillies, chopped
2 cloves garlic, peeled and crushed
100g (3½oz) crushed tomatoes
200g (7oz) caster sugar
80ml (2½fl oz) red wine vinegar

Blend the capsicums, chillies and garlic together. Place the mixture in a saucepan with the rest of the ingredients and cook on top of the stove until thick and syrupy.

TZATZIKI

250ml (9fl oz) natural yoghurt
¼ cup mint leaves, finely chopped
1 clove garlic, crushed
1 tsp lemon juice
zest of ½ lemon, finely chopped
1 tbsp olive oil
sea salt and freshly ground black pepper
    to taste

Blend all the ingredients with a fork until well combined. De-seeded and diced cucumber can be added if desired.

DAHL

1 x 400g (14oz) can lentils
20g (1½oz) butter
1 small onion, finely chopped
1 clove garlic, crushed
½ tsp ground ginger
1 tsp turmeric
¼ tsp garam masala
¼ tsp chilli powder
½ tsp salt
100ml (3½fl oz) coconut cream
  water
1 tsp sugar (optional)

Drain the lentils and put in a small heavy-based saucepan. In another pan, melt the butter and gently sauté the onions and garlic until they are soft, then add all the spices and stir until well combined and fragrant. Add the onions to the lentils. Pour in about ½ cup of water and the coconut cream and simmer—keep stirring until most of the water has reduced so that the lentils don't stick to the bottom. If the dahl is too hot (spicy), you can add sugar to break it down.

- -

GUACAMOLE

1 large avocado, mashed
2 tbsp mayonnaise (see page 124)
½ tsp lime juice
1 red onion, finely chopped
1 long red chilli, deseeded and finely
  chopped
1 clove garlic, crushed
½ tsp sea salt
½ tsp freshly ground black pepper

Thoroughly mash the avocado until creamy. Add the mayonnaise, lime juice, onion, chilli and garlic and season with salt and pepper. Blend and taste—add more of any ingredient to taste. If keeping overnight, squeeze some extra lime juice over the guacamole to stop it from going brown.

- -

OVEN-ROASTED TOMATOES

tomatoes
sea salt and freshly ground black pepper
  to taste
seasoning to taste

Preheat the oven to 140°C (275°F). Quarter some tomatoes (remove the seeds with a teaspoon if you want a drier result), place on a baking tray and season with sea salt and pepper and any dry herb you like or a seasoning like a Tuscan. Roast for 60 to 90 minutes.

HARISSA

*2 roasted red capsicums (peppers) (see
 page 126)*
1 tsp ground cumin
1 tsp ground coriander (cilantro)
½ tsp sambal oelek
4 sprigs flatleaf parsley, finely chopped
*4 sprigs coriander (cilantro), finely
 chopped*
2 cloves garlic
¼ cup olive oil
sea salt to taste

Dice the flesh of the roasted capsicum and blend with all the remaining ingredients into a smooth paste. Put in a sterilised jar and keep in the fridge.

HUMMUS

1 x 400g (14oz) can chickpeas, drained
1 clove garlic, crushed
1 tbsp tahini paste
150ml (5fl oz) olive oil
sea salt and freshly ground black pepper
juice of 1 lime

Put the chick peas, crushed garlic, tahini and half of the oil in a blender and process. Add the salt, pepper and lime juice to taste and the rest of the olive oil. Process the ingredients to a chunky or smooth consistency as you like.

TAHINI YOGHURT SAUCE

2 tbsp natural yoghurt
2 tsp tahini
1 tsp ground cumin
1 tsp honey
juice of 1 lime
sea salt and freshly ground black pepper

Whisk the first five ingredients in a bowl and season with sea salt and pepper to taste.

LIME PICKLE YOGHURT

200g (7oz) natural yoghurt
1 tsp lime pickle chutney

Combine the chutney and yoghurt in a bowl. Store in the refrigerator until ready to use.

RAS EL HANOUT

½ tsp cayenne pepper
½ tsp ground cloves
2 tsp freshly ground black pepper
2 tsp ground allspice
2 tsp ground cumin
2 tsp ground ginger
2 tsp turmeric
2 tsp salt
1 tbsp ground cinnamon
1 tbsp ground coriander (cilantro)
1½ tbsp ground nutmeg

Place all the ingredients in a bowl and mix well. Keep in a sealed jar.

MINT JELLY

300g (10oz) green apples, chopped
8 sprigs mint
water
60ml (2fl oz) white wine vinegar
75g (2½oz) caster sugar

Put the apples in a pan with the roughly chopped leaves from 3 mint sprigs. Pour over enough water to just cover, add the vinegar and bring to the boil. Reduce to a simmer and cook until the apples are soft. Remove from the heat and cool.

Blend the apple until it is smooth, then pour it into a fine sieve over a pan and allow it to filter through for about 15 minutes. Press a little of what is left with the back of a spoon through the sieve. To the sieved liquid, add an equal amount of water, the caster sugar and the rest of the mint leaves, finely chopped. Gently bring the mixture to the boil stirring, then lower to a simmer, until it is reduced by half or until it is a jelly-like consistency. Allow to cool. Pour into a sterilised jar

MAYONNAISE

1 egg
500ml (5fl oz) olive oil
1 tsp white wine vinegar
1 tsp lime juice
1 tsp Dijon mustard
salt and pepper to taste

When making mayonnaise it is best to start with all the ingredients at the same temperature, preferably just out of the fridge.

Using an electric or hand whisk, beat the egg in a bowl until it starts to thicken, then slowly dribble in the olive oil while whisking continuously. As the egg and oil emulsify, slowly add the vinegar (which will loosen the mix) and then more oil until all the oil has been blended in. Then slowly whisk in the Dijon mustard and the lime juice. If the mixture is too loose, whisk in a little more oil until you have the desired consistency. Season with the salt and pepper to taste.

AVOCADO

Mash 1 ripe avocado well and blend with 250ml (8fl oz) mayonnaise.

BASIL

Chop 4 sprigs of basil very finely and blend with 250ml mayonnaise.

BBQ

Mix 75ml (2½fl oz) barbecue sauce together with 250ml (8fl oz) mayonnaise.

PAPRIKA

Combine 20g (1½oz) paprika with 250ml (8fl oz) mayonnaise.

THAI

Remove the spines from 2–3 kaffir lime leaves, roll up together and chop very finely. Very finely chop the softer white part of 1 stick of lemongrass. Blend both with 250ml (8fl oz) mayonnaise.

SALSA VERDE

4 cloves garlic, peeled
50g (1¾oz) capers
150g (5oz) pickled gherkins (in sweet vinegar)
16 sprigs flatleaf parsley
16 sprigs basil
16 sprigs mint
2 tbsp Dijon mustard
200ml (7fl oz) olive oil
sea salt and freshly ground black pepper

Put the finely chopped garlic, capers and gherkins into a blender on pulse and then add the parsley, basil and mint. Add the mustard and slowly add the oil, still pulsing. Sprinkle in the salt and pepper to taste. Pour into a sterilised glass jar and cover with olive oil to seal.

RENDANG SAUCE

100ml (3½fl oz) coconut cream
50ml (1¾fl oz) water
3 tsp brown sugar
2 tsp curry powder
1 tbsp kecap manis

Combine all the ingredients in a saucepan over low heat.

TOMATO BASIL RELISH

1 small onion, diced
1 clove garlic, crushed
1 tbsp olive oil
½ tsp piri piri
1 tsp Moroccan spice
1 tsp sugar
2 tsp red wine vinegar
400g (14oz) crushed tomatoes
3 sprigs basil, chopped

Brown the onions and garlic in the olive oil, add piri piri and Moroccan spice, and then stir for a few minutes. Add sugar and vinegar, stir a few minutes longer, and then add tomatoes. Cook on low heat over a diffuser for 30 minutes.

When cool, add the chopped basil.

RAITA

1 Lebanese cucumber
2 medium tomatoes
1 small red onion
1 long red chilli
1 stem coriander/cilantro (roots and
    leaves)
juice of ½ lime
sea salt and freshly ground black pepper

Peel the cucumber and split in half lengthways. Using a spoon, scrape out the seeds and discard. Cut the tomatoes in half and remove the seeds. Peel the onion. Dice all three ingredients into 5mm cubes and place in a bowl.

Slice the red chilli lengthways and, using a spoon, scrape out the seeds and dice finely. Add to the bowl.

Finely chop the root and stems of the coriander (not the leaves) and add to the bowl. Squeeze over the lime juice and combine. Season with salt and pepper to taste.

ROASTED CAPSICUMS (PEPPERS)

capsicums (peppers)
olive oil to spray

Preheat the oven to 180°C (350°F). Cut the top off the capsicums and remove the seeds and core. Stand them on a baking tray, spray lightly with oil and roast in the oven for 20 minutes. Remove and put in a freezer bag or recycled shopping bag, tie and hang for 15 minutes. You can then easily remove the skins.

TAMARIND SAUCE

50g (1¾oz) palm sugar
25ml (½fl oz) fish sauce
1 tbsp tamarind puree

Put the palm sugar and the fish sauce in a small saucepan over low heat and stir until the palm sugar has dissolved. Allow to cool and stir in the tamarind puree.

OZ RELISH

250ml (8fl oz) tomato basil relish (see
    page 125)
2 tbsp fig jam

Whisk together in a bowl.

ROASTED EGGPLANT (AUBERGINE)

1 large eggplant (aubergine)
olive oil

Preheat the oven to 180°C (350°F). Slice an eggplant into 5mm (¼in) discs, sprinkle with salt and stand in a colander for about 15 minutes, until they sweat. Wash under cold water, pat dry and place on a baking tray with olive oil and roast in the heated oven for 10 minutes each side, adding more oil when turning.

SMOKY EGGPLANT (AUBERGINE) SAUCE

1 large eggplant (aubergine)
1 clove garlic, thinly sliced
1 tsp smoky paprika
1 tsp cumin
1 lime
sea salt and freshly ground black pepper

Preheat the oven to 180°C (350°F). Char the unpeeled eggplant over an open flame (a gas burner on your stove works well) and cut in half lengthways. Crisscross with slits, insert the sliced garlic into the slits and bake for 20 minutes at 180°C (350°F) and then lower the oven to 150°C (300°F) and bake for another 10 minutes, or a little more if the eggplant is not completely soft.

Allow to cool, scoop the flesh out of the skin and put into a food processor. Blend until fairly smooth, pour into a bowl and whisk in the paprika, cumin and then the sea salt and pepper to taste. Finish by squeezing in half or all the lime, again to your taste.

TARTARE SAUCE

220g (7 ½fl oz) mayonnaise (see page 124)
¼ cup sweet gherkins, chopped coarsely
½ cup capers
1 clove garlic, crushed
1 tsp Dijon mustard

Blend all the ingredients together in a blender, but not too smoothly.

INDEX OF RECIPES